Wild Animals

CROCODILE

Lionel Bender

Chrysalis Children's Books

First published in the UK in 2004 by
Chrysalis Children's Books
An imprint of Chrysalis Books Group Plc,
The Chrysalis Building, Bramley Road,
London W10 6SP

ISBN 1 84458 173 X

British Library Cataloguing in Publication Data
for this book is available from the British Library.

Editorial Manager *Joyce Bentley*
Senior Editor *Rasha Elsaeed*
Editorial Assistant *Camilla Lloyd*

Produced by Bender Richardson White
Project Editor *Lionel Bender*
Designer *Ben White*
Production *Kim Richardson*
Picture Researcher *Cathy Stastny*
Cover Make-up *Mike Pilley, Radius*

Printed in China

10 9 8 7 6 5 4 3 2 1

Words in **Bold** can be found in New words on page 31.

Typography *Natascha Frensch*
Read Regular, READ SMALLCAPS and Read Space; European Community Design Registration 2003
and Copyright © Natascha Frensch 2001-2004 **Read Medium, Read Black** and *Read Slanted*
Copyright © Natascha Frensch 2003-2004

READ™ is a revolutionary new typeface that will enchance children's understanding through clear, easily
recognisable character shapes. With its evenly spaced and carefully designed characters, READ™ will help
children at all stages to improve their literacy skills, and is ideal for young readers, reluctant readers and
especially children with dyslexia.

Contents

Crocodiles

A crocodile is a **reptile**. Crocodiles spend part of their time in water and part on land.

There are 14 types of crocodile.
All are strong hunters.

Homes

Crocodiles live in the warmer parts of America, Africa and **South-east Asia.**

Crocodiles live in and around rivers, lakes and **swamps**.

Food

The crocodile is a meat eater.
It eats fish, zebra, birds, deer
and cattle.

A crocodile swallows small **prey** whole. It tears large animals to pieces before eating them.

Hunting

The crocodile usually catches an animal by surprise. It stays still until the animal gets close.

Then it grabs the animal in its teeth and closes its jaws hard.

Daily life

During the day, crocodiles like to sleep in the sun.

They go into the water to cool off. They usually hunt and eat at night.

Senses

The crocodile uses its **senses** of sight and hearing to hunt.

A crocodile has a large tongue and large **nostrils** but its senses of taste and smell are weak.

Weapons

The crocodile uses its strong jaws and sharp teeth to attack and kill enemies.

With a swipe of its thick, heavy tail, the crocodile can hurt and knock over an animal.

Crocodile skin

The crocodile's skin is thick, dry, and **knobbly**. It feels like leather.

The skin is the same colour as mud, sand and soil. This helps the crocodile to hide from its prey.

Baby crocodiles

A mother crocodile buries about 20 eggs in the sand. The sand keeps the eggs warm.

After two to four months,
the baby crocodiles come out
of their eggshells.

Growing up

The mother carries the babies to water in her mouth or on her back.

As the babies swim in the water, they eat insects, frogs and fish. The babies soon grow bigger.

Becoming an adult

Only a small number of baby crocodiles survive. Many are eaten by other animals.

Crocodiles may grow 30 cm in length each year. They take up to 10 years to reach full size.

In danger

Some people kill crocodiles for their meat or skins. They use the skins to make shoes or bags.

Builders take sand from rivers to make roads. This can destroy crocodile homes.

Crocodile care

Scientists study crocodiles to find out how to protect them and make sure they survive.

Crocodile eggs are looked after.
Once the babies break free,
they are put back into the wild.

Quiz

1 How many different types of crocodile are there?

2 In what parts of the world do crocodiles live?

3 When do crocodiles usually hunt?

4 What does a crocodile use as it main weapons?

5 Is a crocodile's skin dry, rough and leathery
or wet and smooth?

6 About how many eggs does a mother crocodile lay?

7 At what age do crocodiles become full size?

8 What do some people use crocodiles' skins for?

The answers are all in this book!

New words

knobbly covered with small, usually round, bumps called knobs.

nostrils openings in the nose through which an animal breathes in and out.

prey an animal that is hunted and killed for food.

reptile cold-blooded animal with a bony skeleton and scaly skin. Reptiles include crocodiles, alligators, lizards, snakes and turtles. Most of them lay eggs on dry land but spend part of their time in water.

senses the way animals find out about their surroundings. Animals have five senses – sight, hearing, smell, taste and touch. The body senses something when it notices it is there.

South-east Asia part of the world between India and China and Australia. It includes such countries as Thailand and Malaysia and islands including Sumatra and Java.

swamps areas of grass and trees, usually in hot countries, in which the ground is always full of water.

Index